Joseph and his Coat of Many Colours

Written by Sasha Morton
Illustrated by Cherie Zamazing

In the town of Canaan, there lived a man named
Jacob who had twelve sons. He loved all of them,
but the eleventh son, Joseph, was his favourite.

Joseph had dreams that he would share with his family.
Sometimes, these dreams made his brothers angry,
because in them Joseph seemed to rule over everyone else.

Joseph's brothers were also very jealous because he had been given a beautiful coat by their father.

One day, when the brothers were tending their sheep, they saw Joseph walking towards them wearing his coloured coat.

4

In anger, the cruel brothers
ripped Joseph's coat from him and
threw him into an old, dry well!

But they were undecided what
to do with their prisoner…

"We must not kill him," said one of the brothers. Then he saw some men approaching with heavily laden camels. "But perhaps we could sell him to these traders?"

So Joseph was dragged from the well and taken to Egypt.

To explain his disappearance, the brothers smeared Joseph's coat with goat's blood, and took it back to their father.

The brothers told Jacob that Joseph was killed by a wild animal. Jacob believed them. He was devastated to have lost his favourite child. Little did Jacob know his son had been sold as a slave!

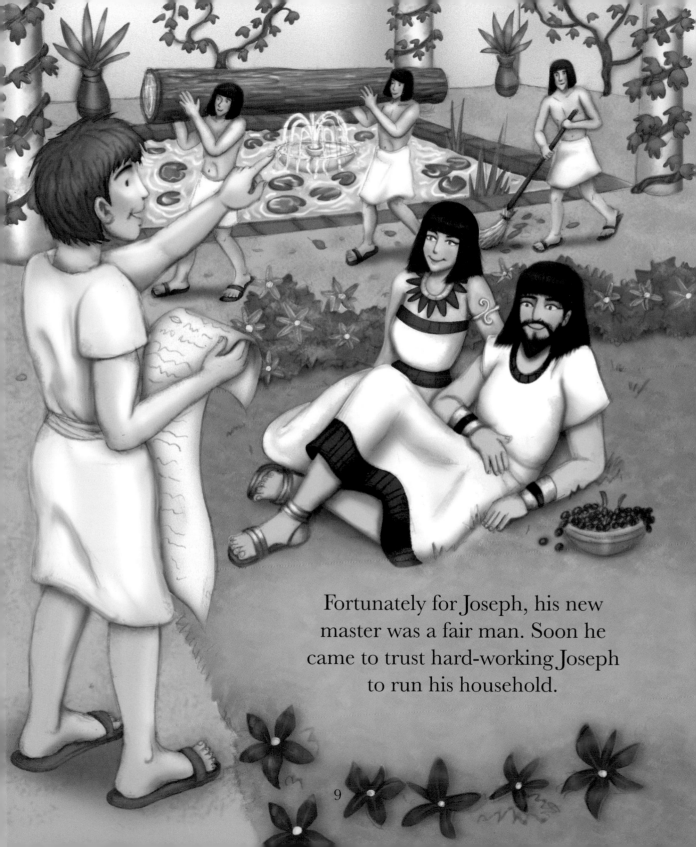

Fortunately for Joseph, his new
master was a fair man. Soon he
came to trust hard-working Joseph
to run his household.

9

Time passed, and Joseph was tricked by a wicked woman and sent to prison. But God continued to help Joseph explain people's dreams. Word of this gift from God spread to the Pharaoh. Troubled by dreams of his own, the Pharaoh sent for Joseph.

"In my dreams, I see seven thin cows eat seven
fat cows," explained the Pharaoh to Joseph.
"Then I see seven ripe ears of corn being swallowed
by seven broken ears of corn. What can this mean?"

Joseph thought the dream had been sent by God,
and told the Pharaoh, "Seven years of plenty are coming,
but they will be followed by seven years of famine.
God wants you to prepare Egypt for what lies ahead."

Joseph continued, "You should store food in the seven good years. This food will feed your people during the seven years of famine."

13

The Pharaoh was so grateful for Joseph's
advice he made him the governor of Egypt.
It was Joseph's job to travel throughout the land,
helping people to get ready for the famine.

14

Once more, Joseph served his master well. He was the
second most important man in Egypt, and became rich
during those seven years of hard work.

And after those seven good years, just as the dream had predicted, the famine began. Thanks to Joseph's planning and storing, no one in Egypt went hungry.

But in Canaan, after two years,
there was nothing left to eat and no crops
would grow in the parched soil.

Joseph's brothers had no choice
but to travel to Egypt to buy grain to
make bread for their starving family.

As the person in charge of selling grain to anyone who came to Egypt in need of food, Joseph watched his brothers bow before him. Not one of them recognised the brother they had sold into slavery.

Joseph said nothing, but sold
them the grain they had come
to him for. He knew that the
famine would continue, and that
they would return again.

When Jacob sent his sons to Egypt the next time, Joseph stood before them and said, "I am Joseph. Is my father still alive?"

All of the brothers were amazed to see Joseph was still alive.
They wept and said sorry for what they had done
to him. With a glad heart, Joseph forgave them.

"What happened to me was all part of God's plan to
save many lives," he explained. "There are five more years of
famine to come, but I have stored enough food for everyone.
Do not blame yourselves for what you did."

The Pharaoh was so grateful to Joseph for keeping his people safe from hunger, he told him his family could come and live in Egypt too. Joseph proudly sent his brothers home to Canaan to bring back their father and their families.

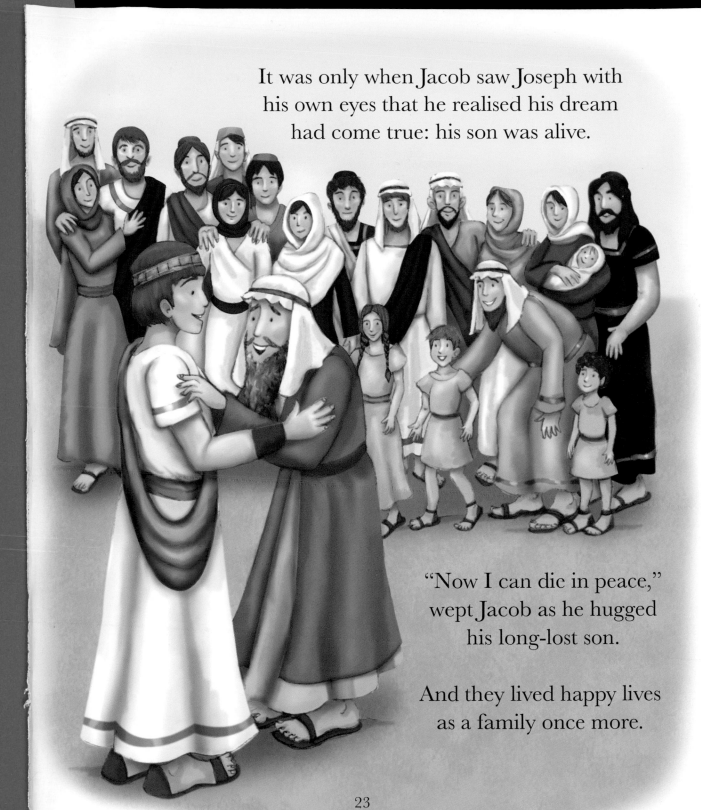

It was only when Jacob saw Joseph with his own eyes that he realised his dream had come true: his son was alive.

"Now I can dic in peace," wept Jacob as he hugged his long-lost son.

And they lived happy lives as a family once more.

An Hachette UK Company
www.hachette.co.uk

First published in Great Britain in 2014 by Ticktock,
an imprint of Octopus Publishing Group Ltd
Endeavour House
189 Shaftesbury Avenue
London
WC2H 8JY
www.octopusbooks.co.uk
www.ticktockbooks.co.uk

ISBN 978 1 84898 935 1

A CIP record for this book is available from the British Library.

Printed and bound in China

10 9 8 7 6 5 4 3 2 1

With thanks to: Jana Burson

Series Editor: Lucy Cuthew Design: Advocate Art
Publisher: Tim Cook Managing Editor: Karen Rigden
Assistant Production Manager: Lucy Carter